A Family in West Germany

LIBRARY OF CONGRESS CATALOGING IN PUBLICATION DATA

Adler, Ann.
   A family in West Germany.

   Rev. ed. of: German family. 1984.
   Summary: Describes the life of an eleven-year-old
girl who lives with her family in Mainburg, Germany.
   1. Germany (West)—Social life and customs—Juvenile
literature. 2. Children—Germany (West)—Juvenile
literature. 3. Family—Germany (West)—Juvenile
literature. [1. Germany (West)—Social life and
customs]
I. Fairclough, Chris, ill. II. Adler, Ann. German
family. III. Title.
DD2603.A35 1985   943.0-87'8   85-6981
ISBN 0-8225-1658-6 (lib. bdg.)

Manufactured in the United States of America

1 2 3 4 5 6 7 8 9 10 95 94 93 92 91 90 89 88 87 86 85

A Family in West Germany

Ann Adler

Photographs by Chris Fairclough

Lerner Publications Company • Minneapolis

main roads
low ground
high ground
mountains
100km
50 miles
N

Renate Blattner is 11 years old and lives in Mainburg, a small town almost 40 miles (60 kilometers) from Munich. Munich is the third largest city in West Germany and the capital of Bavaria. Bavaria is one of 11 states of West Germany.

Renate, whose nickname is Reni, lives with her parents, Hans and Helga, and her brother, Christian. He is 13 years old. Reni's family lives in an apartment building. Their apartment has two bedrooms, a living room, a kitchen, and a bathroom.

Because they want more room, they are building a new house in a nearby village. There Reni will have her own bedroom.

But she will miss seeing her grandparents everyday. They are her mother's parents and live in the apartment above them.

NORTH RHINE WESTPHALIA

Dortmund

Düsseldorf

Cologne

Bonn

HESSE

MOSELLE

Frankfurt

RHINELAND-PALATINATE

R RHINE

Stuttgart

BADEN-WÜRTTEMBERG

Ulm

R

DANUBE

Wolnzach

Mainburg

Sandelshausen

BAVARIA

Nuremberg

Munich

Salzburg

Basel

Zurich

SWITZERLAND

The Alps

AUSTRIA

CZECHOSLOVAKIA

Inset map

NORWAY

SWEDEN

GREAT BRITAIN

IRELAND

DENMARK

NORTH SEA

BALTIC SEA

POLAND

London

HOLLAND

Berlin

WEST GERMANY

EAST GERMANY

Paris

FRANCE

CZECHO-SLOVAKIA

Munich

AUSTRIA

ATLANTIC OCEAN

SWITZ.

ITALY

YUGOSLAVIA

SPAIN

MEDITERRANEAN

Reni's father is building the family's new house himself. He works on it every afternoon after his regular job and also on Saturdays. Reni's mother worries that he works too hard and doesn't relax enough. But everyone agrees that all the work will be worth it when the house is ready.

Sometimes relatives and family friends help her father on the house. Her grandfather and uncle laid the bricks for the first floor of the house, and even Reni helped spread the mortar. There is always a job for anyone who has time to work. It will be at least six more months before the house is ready to move into.

The new house is in Sandelshausen, the village next to Mainburg. Reni and her brother will still be going to the same schools in Mainburg. They'll just have to get up earlier to catch their school buses.

Now the bus picks up Reni at 7:45 A.M. She waits for the bus at the same corner as her friend Brigitte. They always sit next to each other on the bus.

School starts at 8:00 A.M. and ends at 1:00 P.M. There aren't any classes in the afternoon, but there are activities. On Mondays, Reni stays at school for a dance and keep-fit class. She does lots of different exercises and learns the latest dances.

Reni's school is called a *Hauptschule* (HOWPT shoola). This is her first year there. The building is very modern and much bigger than her old school was. It has 800 students. All the classrooms are grouped around a big hall. On rainy days, the students sit in the hall during their breaks.

Christian's school is called a *Gymnasium* (gim NAH zee um). His school is right next to Reni's, but she never sees him during the day. He leaves home earlier than she does and rides a different bus.

Reni is in the sixth grade, and her teacher is Mrs. Greilinger. The class learns German, math, physics, geography, English, history, and biology. Reni's favorite subject is geography, and she has a special set of colored pencils just for drawing maps.

Every morning, the class has five or six lessons. There is a five-minute break between lessons and a long break at 9:30 A.M. In nice weather, everyone spends the long break outside in the schoolyard. Sometimes Reni brings a sandwich and a carton of milk from home for the break. Otherwise she buys something to eat at school.

Reni's father leaves for work very early in the morning, when the rest of the family is still asleep. He works in Munich and must be there by 7:00 A.M. Many people from Mainburg work in Munich because there aren't many jobs in Mainburg.

Mr. Blattner works at Bavarian Motor Works, the company that makes BMW cars. Reni's family has a BMW.

One of Mr. Blattner's friends works for Volkswagen, another German car company. He and Reni's father often argue about which cars are best.

Reni's father doesn't use his car to go to work, though. A company bus picks him up in the morning and brings him home in the afternoon.

The BMW plant produces about 900 cars a day. The cars are sold in Germany and all over the world. Over 25,000 people work for the company.

The offices are in a very tall building. From the top, you can see how enormous the BMW plant is. If you look out of the office windows the other way, you can see Munich's Olympic Stadium, where the Olympics were held in 1972. Now anyone can use the swimming pools and tennis courts there.

Big soccer matches are held in the stadium. (The Germans call this game football.) Mr. Blattner and Christian always go to watch when their favorite football team, *TSV München 1860*, plays there.

Reni's father used to work on the production line, where the cars are built. Now he teaches apprentices, people who are being trained at the plant. There are more than 600 apprentices at BMW. Most of them are men, but there are some women, too.

In the first year, Mr. Blattner teaches the apprentices metalwork. He shows them how to cut and shape metal and how to drill holes in it. The apprentices have to know all about the different tools that are used for working with metal. Later on, they learn all about car engines.

The apprentices must understand how an engine works. They have to be able to take one apart and put it back together again. They also learn how the different parts of a car are put together on the production line—how the hood is fitted, how a door is built, how the seats are installed, and much more.

At the end of the third year, the apprentices are given an exam. Those who pass are qualified to work as car mechanics, fitters, welders, or metalworkers. Some stay and work for BMW, and others find jobs elsewhere. One of Mr. Blattner's former students works at BMW as a fitter. Here he is helping to test the engine of a new car on the production line.

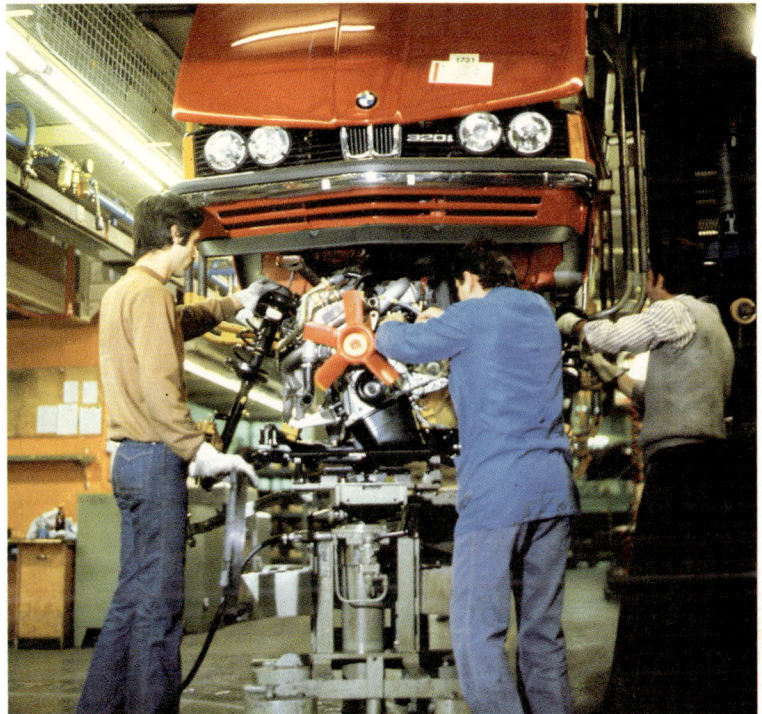

13

Reni's father returns home from work at 4 P.M. He has sandwiches for lunch, so her mother cooks a hot meal for him in the evening. The rest of the family eats their main meal at lunchtime, when Reni and Christian get home from school.

Reni's mother spends her mornings shopping, doing the housework, and cooking. She also grows beautiful flowers and has a vegetable garden in the back yard.

After lunch, Christian and Reni take turns doing dishes. Then they do their homework.

They work in the living room because their room is too small. They have homework every day.

Christian loves to do woodwork. He has built many things, including a model airplane and some loudspeaker boxes. He has a workbench in the basement and disappears down there as soon as his homework is done.

Reni likes to ride her bicycle. When she has finished her homework, she bikes down to the fountain in the main square to meet her friends.

Sometimes, Reni and her friend Susanne visit Susanne's grandfather. He is a farmer and is always working, even on Saturday. But often he will stop long enough to give Susanne and Reni a ride on his tractor.

Susanne's grandfather keeps cows and pigs on his farm. He also grows hops, which grow on vines. When the hops are ripe, he picks them and lets them dry out. Then he sells them to a brewery.

Hops are used for brewing beer. There are hop fields all around Mainburg. It is one of the biggest hop growing areas in Europe.

Reni and her friends also enjoy going for walks in the forest. With its tall pine trees, the forest is a good place for playing *Verstecken*, or hide-and-seek.

In the evening, Reni and Christian usually stay home and watch television. There are three German television channels, but Reni's family can also watch the Austrian programs. The border between Germany and Austria isn't far from Mainburg.

Reni's favorite program is a weekly show with all the new pop songs. Christian likes to watch sports programs. When there's an important football match on TV, the whole family watches it.

On Saturday, Reni helps her mother with the shopping. They must do it all in the morning, because the stores close at lunchtime. During the week, they stay open until 6:00 or 6:30.

Reni tries to get to the bakery early on Saturday. If she arrives too late, many things are already gone. Bäckeri Müller, where Reni shops, sells all kinds of bread—long loaves of white bread, round loaves of sourdough, dark loaves of pumpernickel, and small hard rolls. Reni usually buys a *Bretzel*, a large pretzel, to eat right away.

While Reni is at the bakery, her mother goes to the butcher. There she can buy pork chops, roasts, and other kinds of meat.

The butcher also has a large selection of sausages and cold meats, called *Aufschnitt* (OWF schnit). Reni's mother often buys smoked or cooked ham, which the butcher slices for her.

Three popular kinds of sausage are *Weisswurst* (VICE vurst), a long white sausage, *Servelat* (ZAIR ve lot), and *Würstchen* (VURST chen), or frankfurters. The sausages usually have to be cooked, but some can be eaten cold.

On Saturdays, Reni gets three *Deutschemarks* (DOYCH marks), her weekly allowance. She often saves this money. Sometimes, though, her mother lets her go to a cafe with her friends. There they order wonderful things to eat and drink—ice cream topped with whipped cream, fancy cakes, and fizzy drinks. Even the smallest cafe in Mainburg has at least ten different kinds of cake to choose from. Reni usually spends her whole allowance in one visit to the cafe.

19

Sunday is the only day of the week that Reni's whole family can have breakfast together. They usually eat bread with jam or slices of cold sausage, and they drink coffee with milk. Once in a while, they even have a piece of cake.

After Sunday breakfast, Reni and Christian go to church. At Christmas, Easter, and other important holidays, Mr. and Mrs. Blattner also go to church. But usually they like to stay home and relax. Reni's mother says it is the only time that they can have a quiet time together.

Like most people in Bavaria, the Blattners are Catholic. There are three churches in Mainburg. Reni and Christian go to the biggest church, which is located right on the main square.

Reni often wears her *Dirndl* to church. It's a traditional Bavarian dress made of blue material with a fine pattern. The sleeves are white lace, and a red apron covers the dress.

Every Sunday noon, the Blattners have a big meal. Often, Reni and Christian's grandparents come downstairs to eat with them.

Their meal usually begins with soup. A typical meal might include meat with gravy, potatoes, vetegables, *Knödl* (K'NO dul), and a salad. *Knödl* are a special kind of dumpling made of bread. For dessert, there is a fruit trifle, which is a combination of pudding, cake, and fruit.

Reni's father was born in Czechoslovakia. He came to Mainburg with his mother when he was a very young boy. His mother died a few years ago. Every weekend, he visits her grave and puts fresh flowers on it. Reni and Christian go with him to light a candle.

Reni's mother was born in Mainburg and has never lived anywhere else. Many of her relatives live nearby and the families often visit one another.

Reni's aunt and uncle have a baby girl. When Reni's aunt is busy, she leaves the baby with Reni's grandmother. Then Reni goes upstairs to play with the baby and help take care of her.

Every fall, there is a famous fair in Munich. It's called *Oktoberfest*. Thousands of people from all over the world come to Munich, (or München, as it is called in German) for the fair, which lasts for two weeks. Reni's family spends a day at the fair every year.

They drive into Munich on the *Autobahn* (OW toe bon), the German version of the freeway. There is usually no speed limit on the *Autobahn*. Drivers often go 80 miles an hour (130 kilometers per hour) and faster.

There is a lot of traffic in Munich, and it is hard to find a place to park. For that reason, Reni's father parks the car on the outskirts of Munich. The family rides the underground train into the center of the city. The underground was built only a few years ago. Munich also has trams and buses. Trams drive along the street on tracks and are attached to wires overhead.

The underground stations are very modern. There are no ticket offices. Instead, you buy your ticket from a machine. But first you must look at the map to find out what zone you are in and what zone you are going to. Then you know what kind of ticket to buy. Even people who live in the city often have to do this.

25

At the Oktoberfest, the fairground is enormous. Reni and Christian stick close to their parents so that they don't get lost. There are roller-coasters, bumper cars, swings, ghost trains, and many other kinds of rides.

All of the rides are expensive, and Reni and Christian choose carefully which they will go on. They want to save some money to spend on other things at the fair.

There are many stands that sell all kinds of food: grilled sausages, sandwiches with pickled herrings, ice cream, cotton candy, sugared almonds, and cold drinks. There are also big tents where adults can sit at long tables and drink beer.

Christian and Reni try as many different foods as they can. Soon Christian has spent all his money, but Reni still has a little bit left.

Her last purchase is a *Lebkuchenherz* (LABE kooken hairtz), a honey cake shaped like a heart. The cake is decorated with sugar and usually has a funny saying on it.

Reni is too full to eat her *Lebkuchenherz* right away, so she hangs it around her neck. She and Christian go on one more ride, and then it's time to go back to Mainburg. Everyone is tired, but all agree that it has been a wonderful day.

West Germany and East Germany

When talking about Germany today, it's very important to say *which* Germany you mean—East or West. At one time they were part of the same country, but they are now two separate and very different countries.

West Germany is over twice the size of East Germany and has about four times as many people. The official name of West Germany is *Bundesrepublik Deutschland*, or Federal Republic of Germany.

The official name of East Germany is *Deutsche Demokratische Republik*, or German Democratic Republic.

Berlin used to be the capital city of Germany. When the country was divided, so was Berlin. A wall was built to separate East Berlin from West Berlin. East Berlin belongs to East Germany and is its capital. Although it sits right in the middle of East Germany, West Berlin is an independent city whose citizens are part of West Germany.

Facts about West Germany

Capital: Bonn

Language: German

Form of Money: the Deutsche mark

Area: 96,000 square miles (248,651 square kilometers)

The United States, including Alaska and Hawaii, is almost 38 times as big as Germany.

Population: about 60 million people

The population of West Germany is about one-fourth that of the United States.

NORTH
AMERICA

SOUTH
AMERICA

EUROPE

West Germany

ASIA

AFRICA

AUSTRALIA

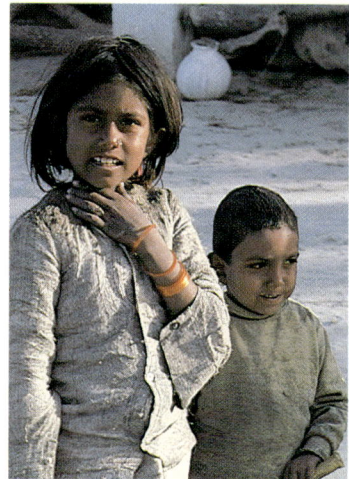

Families the World Over

Some children in foreign countries live like you do. Others live very differently. In these books, you can meet children from all over the world. You'll learn about their games and schools, their families and friends, and what it's like to grow up in a faraway land.

A FAMILY IN CHINA   A FAMILY IN PAKISTAN

A FAMILY IN EGYPT   A FAMILY IN SRI LANKA

A FAMILY IN FRANCE   A FAMILY IN WEST GERMANY

A FAMILY IN INDIA   AN ABORIGINAL FAMILY

A FAMILY IN JAMAICA   AN ARAB FAMILY

A FAMILY IN NIGERIA   AN ESKIMO FAMILY

Lerner Publications Company
241 First Avenue North
Minneapolis, Minnesota 55401